THE FIFTIES

THE FIFTIES

Photographs of America by   EVE ARNOLD

CORNELL CAPA

BRUCE DAVIDSON

ELLIOTT ERWITT

BURT GLINN

ERNST HAAS

ERICH HARTMANN

BOB HENRIQUES

COSTA MANOS

WAYNE MILLER

INGE MORATH

DENNIS STOCK

of MAGNUM

Introduction by   JOHN CHANCELLOR

Pantheon Books

New York

All rights reserved under International and Pan-American Copyright
Conventions. Published in the United States by Pantheon Books,
a division of Random House, Inc., New York, and simultaneously in
Canada by Random House of Canada Limited, Toronto.

Library of Congress Cataloging in Publication Data
Main entry under title:

The Fifties : photographs of America.

    1. United States—Description and travel—1940–
1960—Views.   2. United States—Social life and
customs—1945–1970—Pictorial works.   I. Arnold, Eve.
E169.02.F444   1985   779′.9973921   84-18948

ISBN 0-394-54064-6
ISBN 0-394-72720-7 (pbk.)

Manufactured in the United States of America
First Edition

For Magnum: Lee Jones, Editor
                Tom Brazil, Associate Editor
Book designed by Homans│Salsgiver

Frontispiece:
View from car window.
Wyoming, 1954.
Elliott Erwitt.

THE FIFTIES

THE FIFTIES

**These are the tranquillized *Fifties*,
and I am forty. Ought I to regret my seedtime?**

So wrote the poet Robert Lowell a quarter of a century ago.

The tranquillized Fifties. It was a fashionable view. Eisenhower on the golf course, or in the hospital, drowsing as his big-business buddies carved up the country. Fins on cars. Hula Hoops. A country entranced by materialism. The age of the expense account.

There was a lot more to it than that. The decade produced heroes, villains, and buffoons in great numbers. It had moments of extraordinary drama, sadness, and delight. Robert Lowell, at forty, may have found it tranquillized, but those of us in our twenties didn't regret our seedtime.

The Fifties included a bitter war in Asia, which at times threatened an American defeat; and a tide of witch-hunting at home which at times seemed to threaten our basic liberties. But it was better than the brutal Thirties, the wartime Forties, the convulsive Sixties, or the tragic Seventies.

The decade had two presidents, Truman and Eisenhower. Neither man, while in office, was regarded as having much style or brainpower. We now know that both were far better than we guessed at the time, and much better presidents than most of their successors.

Eisenhower was a Republican who enjoyed the company of tycoons. He talked about "dynamic conservatism." The Republicans were in the White House for the first time in twenty years, and the conservative wing of the party was strong. Yet, during his eight years in office, Ike either maintained or expanded all the significant programs of the New Deal.

Black Americans (then called Negroes — you didn't call a black a black in those days) began the Fifties almost completely segregated, in everything from water fountains to education. The decade brought about considerable progress and instilled great hope for equal rights, thanks mainly to the Supreme Court and the Chief Justice appointed by Eisenhower, Earl Warren. Warren's liberalism surprised Eisenhower, but Ike did nothing to block the court's landmark school-desegregation decision of 1954. No Congress had passed a civil rights law affecting black voting rights since 1870. One was passed in 1957. Eisenhower was maddeningly slow on civil rights, but what happened while he was in office made possible the accomplishments of men like Martin Luther King, Jr., and Thurgood Marshall in the Sixties.

When the demagogic governor of Arkansas, Orval Faubus, stirred up mobs in Little Rock against the desegregation of Central High

School, Eisenhower landed the 82nd Airborne Division to keep order and enforce the law. It was the first operation by federal troops in a southern city since Reconstruction.

Neither Truman nor Eisenhower was able to control a venomous tide of ideological witch-hunting that started at the end of World War II. The United States had gone on a Red-menace binge after World War I and it did the same thing thirty years later. The blacklists, purges, and loyalty oaths intensified when the new decade began. Many people had genuine concerns about subversion. Alger Hiss, who had been on the American diplomatic team at the Yalta Conference, was convicted of perjury in 1950 on charges relating to the Communist Party. Julius and Ethel Rosenberg were arrested that year for passing atomic data to the Russians and later executed, despite widespread protests. The Russians tested an atomic bomb, and most Americans believed they had stolen our nuclear secrets. China had fallen to the Communists. North Korea had invaded South Korea. Americans, at no little cost, had beaten the Nazis. Would they now have to defeat world Communism? Were there traitors in Washington? It was a real question in 1950.

Senator Joseph McCarthy of Wisconsin cast his feral gaze on all this and began waving lists of what he described as known Communists in the federal government. With a few courageous exceptions, the national press gave deadpan credence to his vaporous ravings. Distinguished politicians, including Eisenhower, shunned his company but wouldn't speak out against his excesses. Truman, on the other hand, called him a pathological liar. McCarthy and his two young accomplices, Roy Cohn and David Schine, were able to terrorize the State Department and the federal bureacracy for several years. When McCarthy tried to terrorize the U.S. Army to get special privileges for Schine, who had been drafted, the Eisenhower administration, the Senate, and public opinion finally moved against him. Edward R. Murrow went on television with a carefully worded denunciation, but CBS gave McCarthy equal time for rebuttal. The senator was censured by the Senate in 1954 and died in 1957, his only legacy the ugly word *McCarthyism.* He had helped create a shameful civil war between different groups of Americans. Walt Kelly, creator of the liberal comic strip *Pogo,* wrote, "We has met the enemy, and it is us."

If World War II was the last of the "good" wars, Korea may have been the first of the "bad" wars. It was never declared a war by the Congress, and it was fought in a far-off place for goals that were sometimes unclear. Parents had a hard time understanding why their sons died. Korea bears some resemblance to Vietnam. But there is a difference. Fifty-eight thousand Americans died in Vietnam, and it tore the country apart. Almost as many died in Korea — fifty-three thousand — but the country held together in the Fifties.

It was a time in which Harry Truman, an unpopular president overseeing an unpopular war, could fire one of the most famous generals in history and get away with it. Truman sacked General of the Army Douglas MacArthur in 1951 for what amounted to insufferable insubordination (MacArthur, commander in Korea, kept advocating an invasion of China). MacArthur returned to the United States to the cheers of multitudes, traveled slowly across the country speaking to enormous crowds, and told the Congress, "Old soldiers never die; they just fade away." Which is just what the American people let him do.

The Korean War may have been easier to bear because the economy at home was so strong. The Fifties were the centerpiece of what has been called the longest cycle of capitalist expansion in history. The boom had begun when World War II ended and it would last more than twenty years. There were recessions, and times of high unemployment, but the American people were essentially prosperous throughout the decade.

America was growing, learning, and discovering. In 1952, a terrible epidemic of poliomyelitis crippled thousands and took the lives of thirty-three hundred victims, but later that year Jonas Salk tested his vaccine against polio, and it worked. American scientists won more Nobel Prizes in the Fifties than in the Sixties. Something was being invented every minute.

It was, above all, a time of hope. We believed Henry Luce when he said it was the American Century. We made jokes about the ads that spoke of better living through chemistry, but in our hearts we knew it was true. The great engine of American productivity was exporting growth to Western Europe and Japan. American films and musical comedies were the envy of the world. American art and architecture were unsurpassed.

Yes, the Russians in 1957 had put a sphere about the size of a basketball in orbit around the earth. But we would catch them. We were ahead of the Russians in everything else. Nikita Khrushchev said in 1956, "We will bury you," but no one believed that. America in the Fifties really was the future.

Another way to look at the 1950s, and at these photographs, is to see the decade as a great passage from one style of American life to another, a journey not so much in time as in culture.

When World War II ended, the United States looked as it had looked in the 1930s. Very few civilian products were made during the war. When it ended, there were no new cars, people's houses and kitchens and bathrooms were prewar, the newspapers, magazines, and radio programs were largely unchanged. The look and feel of the countryside, of the big cities and small towns, was very much of the Thirties. At the beginning of the Fifties, America in the summertime was a country of ceiling fans, pitchers of icewater, and dusty roads.

Sears, Roebuck was doing a brisk business selling parts for Model T and Model A Fords, and it seemed as though every other farm was using one of the old cars.

That began to change as the Fifties got underway, but the change was gradual. It took time in a country of 150,000,000 people to get new stoves, clothes, houses, and cars to everybody. And there was a great demand for new products, such as air conditioning, which was nonexistent in ordinary homes before the the war. When the decade began, there were no self-service elevators, no direct-mail telephones, no computers, no credit cards, no transistor radios, no diet drinks; practically nobody smoked filter cigarettes. All that had changed by the end of the decade, but when it began, it was a world in which the telephone operator said, "Number, please?" and the elevator operator asked you for your floor.

Television existed only on a local level in 1950. The networks were not able to send live pictures across the country until the following year. Most TV sets were in saloons. The programs were aimed at saloon audiences: wrestling, and ladies with large bosoms on variety shows. As the decade began, only 9 percent of American homes were able to receive television pictures. By 1960, the figure had risen to 87 percent.

The patterns of life in the early years of the Fifties were pretty much what they had been twenty years before. There was a great deal of small-town, Main Street America in those days. The huge migration of the rural poor to the cities was only getting started. The older suburbs were still havens for the well-to-do. Levittowns, suburban bedroom communities for workers, were being built on farmland.

Air traffic was growing, but it took a long time to get somewhere in a twin-engine DC-3. Jet travel was not introduced until 1957. In the early years of the decade, railroads were still the way to go. That included trains like the *Super Chief* and the *20th Century Limited,* which emphasized luxury. Train stations in big cities were rather grand – not just clean and free of derelicts, but places of business and fashion. Reporters went to train stations to interview celebrities. Men wore hats and vests. Women wore gloves, fur jackets, and veils.

If you weren't looking for work, black, or getting shot at in Korea, it was a very nice time. The country felt young. The future was full of promise. You knew where things stood and you knew who you were.

Knowing where things stood meant understanding and agreeing to what the sociologists were beginning to call the power structure. In those days, noted clergymen got their important sermons reported in the papers. Editors paid attention to statements by spokesmen for big business, big labor, and the presidents of big universities. In the Fifties, the elders exercised authority, and few objected.

The liberation of women had not begun, but the stirrings were there. Simone de Beauvoir's book *The Second Sex* was published in translation in 1953. Karl Menninger, the psychiatrist, described it as "a pretentious and inflated tract on feminism," but Philip Wylie, the author, called it "one of the few great books of our time." About three out of four married women did not work, and women with children were expected to stay at home.

There were children everywhere. By 1956, most of them seemed to be about ten years old. Their daddies and mommies had got together the year after the war, when the baby boom started. There also seemed to be an awful lot of high school kids born before the war began – proud young boys with crewcuts, girls in skirts and bobbysox. Blue jeans were just overalls, and overalls were for farmers. Jeans were Tobacco Road, buddy, and Tobacco Road was out, among the upwardly mobile, sexually ambitious kids of the Fifties.

Sex. It was there all the time, just about everywhere you looked. Jayne Mansfield, John Wayne (who was quite a lot younger then, no kidding), Marilyn Monroe, the boy next door, the matron across the dinner table. Sexually, Americans were drawn as tight as the string on a crossbow. There was a general sense of anticipation, a feeling that delicious experiences were just around the corner. For the young, there were masculine dreams of career and success, feminine dreams of children and a home, but before that – oh, joy! – there would be the end of innocence. And it was all the more appetizing because there was no open promiscuity. The Sixties would bring that. In the Fifties, you pretended that the old proprieties still held, but you went pretty far on the first date.

If there were an index here, it would read: "*Sex* – see *Automobile*." "*Automobile* – see *Sex*." We had gone from Andy Hardy's front porch to the back seat of dad's Chevy. In the Thirties, a few rich kids necked in convertibles. In the Fifties, nearly everybody had a car. No generation of Americans had ever owned so many motorcars; no generation of children had ever had such opportunities to be alone together. The car was a symbol of freedom; when James Dean made the movie *Rebel Without a Cause,* he used his own 1949 black Mercury coupe in the film.

The Fifties produced the great income shift to the young. Parents in the Thirties battled the Depression; in the Forties they coped with meat stamps and gasoline rationing. There wasn't much to spare. But in the Fifties, kids were given more money to spend, on things like records and phonographs. Especially on records and phonographs. From 1952 until 1960, manufacturers produced more than twenty-six million record players. The long-playing record was invented, which changed listening habits, a lot of things changed: Teeny-boppers emerged as a significant component of the American economy. The young became consumers as they had never been before, in any country. Kids began spending billions on entertainment, and platoons of savvy grownups figured out ways they could spend even more. It was one of the most profound changes in American life.

The decade had begun with the sounds of the big bands. It ended with rock and roll at full volume. America invented rock and roll in the mid-Fifties and exported it to the world. Rock returned with the Beatles. With that came a new style for the young, long hair and guitars. Jeans, Frisbees, and drugs would soon follow. The whole loose, unstructured youth culture was on its way.

So much had changed by the time the decade ended. The cities were starting to fall apart, the suburbs were filling up, and the countryside was being emptied.

America was becoming a different nation, tied no longer to the certainties of the past. The old consensus was breaking up. Those years were not a tranquillized pause in history, but a laboratory in which the future was invented and tested. Before we got to the Fifties, we had lived in one kind of country. When the decade ended, we were on our way somewhere else.

Jack Kerouac, the bard of the Beat Generation, wrote in 1957,

Where we going, man?
I don't know, but we gotta go.

John Chancellor
Pound Ridge, New York
October 1984

Bobbysoxers.
Michigan City, Indiana, 1954.
Cornell Capa.
(*Life* magazine © Time Inc.)

Saying grace.
Lebo, Kansas, 1950.
Wayne Miller.

President Eisenhower.
Gettysburg, Pennsylvania, 1959.
Burt Glinn.

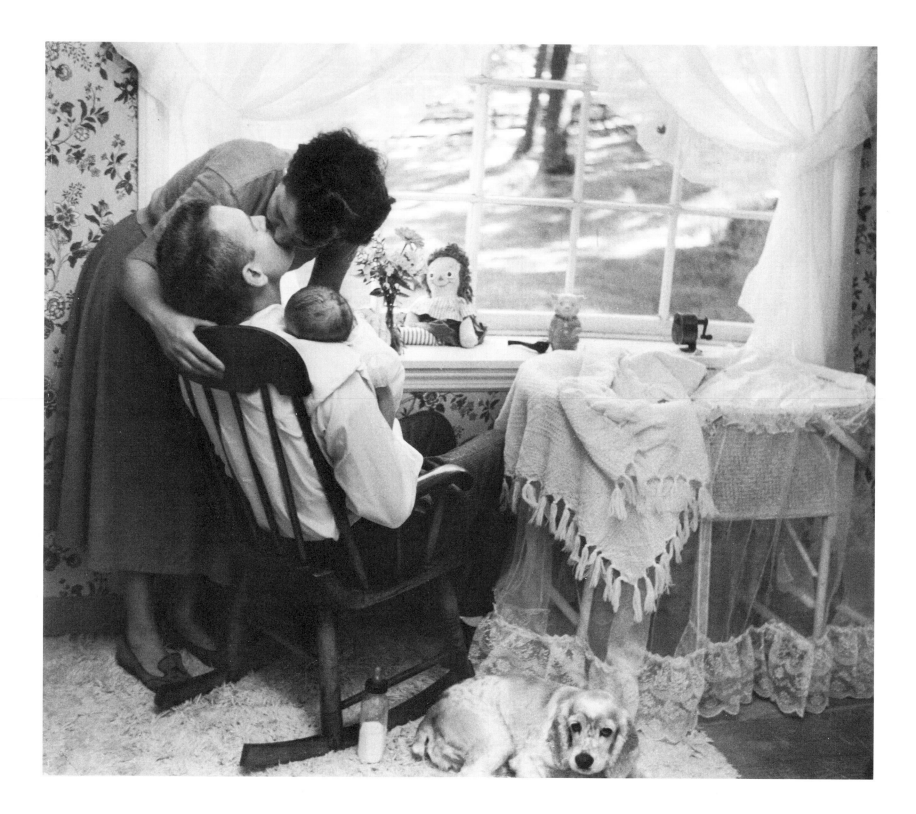

Parents with new baby.
Long Island, New York, 1955.
Eve Arnold.

Young mother.
New Rochelle, New York, 1955.
Elliott Erwitt.

Methodist Sunday school.
Lebo, Kansas, 1950.
Wayne Miller.

Flag Day ceremony.
Orinda, California, 1956.
Wayne Miller.

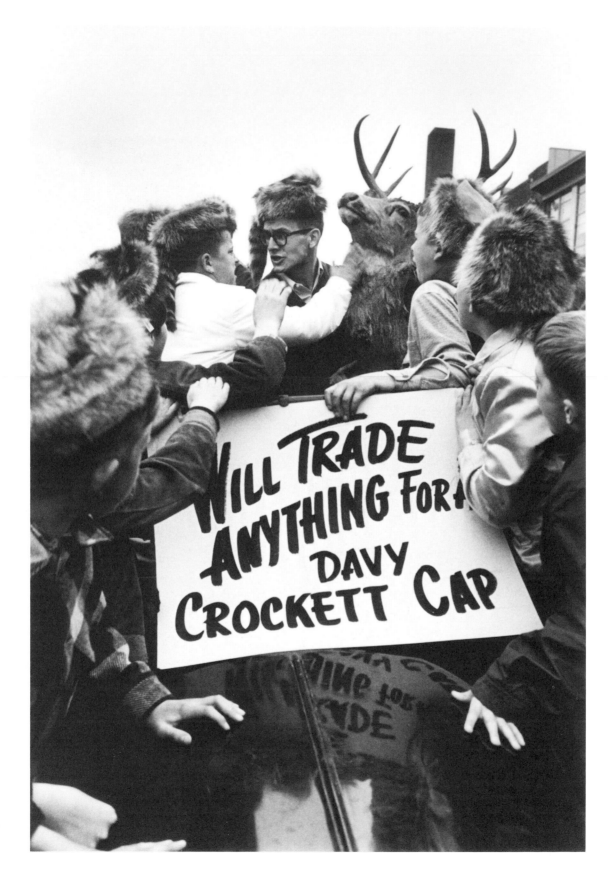

Davy Crockett mania.
Seattle, Washington, 1955.
Burt Glinn.

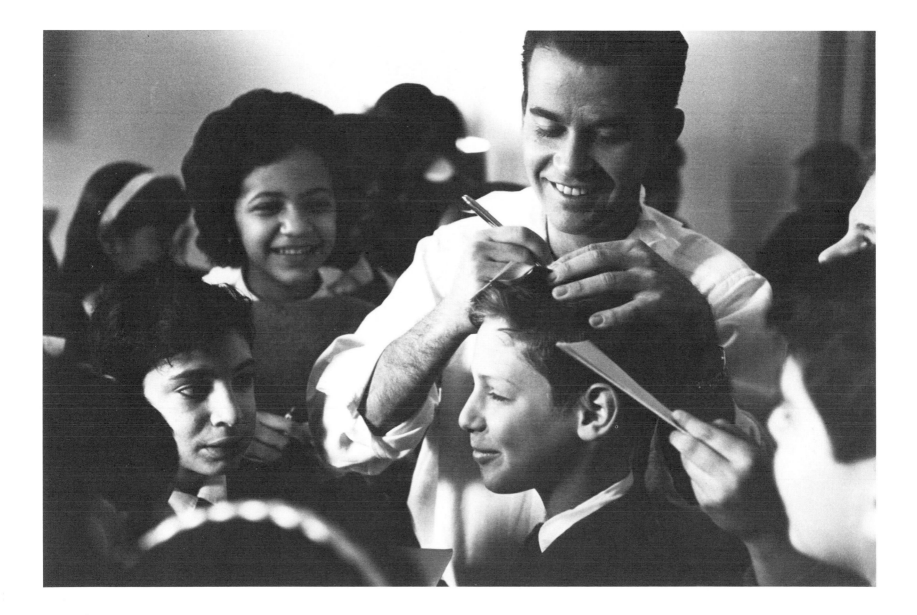

Dick Clark and admirers.
New York City, 1959.
Wayne Miller.

Hula Hoop.
Columbia, South Carolina, 1958.
Costa Manos.

Backyard.
Orinda, California, 1954.
Wayne Miller.

Beach scene.
Long Island, New York, 1954.
Ernst Haas.

Innertubing party on the canals.
Seattle, Washington, 1953.
Burt Glinn.

Teenager.

Michigan City, Indiana, 1954.

Cornell Capa.

(*Life* magazine © Time Inc.)

Flying saucers.
New York City, 1959.
Burt Glinn.

Graduation ceremonies.
Orinda, California, 1957.
Wayne Miller.

First formal, before the dance.
Michigan City, Indiana, 1954.
Cornell Capa.
(*Life* magazine © Time Inc.)

The bunny hop.
Michigan City, Indiana, 1954.
Cornell Capa.
(*Life* magazine © Time Inc.)

Exeter Academy students.
Exeter, New Hampshire, 1956.
Elliott Erwitt.

American Bandstand.
Philadelphia, Pennsylvania, 1958.
Bruce Davidson.

Cheerleader.
Gulfport, Mississippi, 1954.
Elliott Erwitt.

High school football game.
Seattle, Washington, 1955.
Burt Glinn.

High school football game.
Seattle, Washington, 1955.
Burt Glinn.

Dartmouth College.
Hanover, New Hampshire, 1956.
Elliott Erwitt.

Installation of Clark Kerr as president.
University of California at Berkeley, 1958.
Wayne Miller.

Brown University class of 1955.
Providence, Rhode Island, 1955.
Elliott Erwitt.

Working on the car.
Connecticut, 1958.
Cornell Capa.

Recess, the day the high school was integrated.
Little Rock, Arkansas, 1957.
Burt Glinn.

Recess.
Little Rock, Arkansas, 1957.
Burt Glinn.

High school students during the first week of integration.
Little Rock, Arkansas, 1957.
Burt Glinn.

Supporters of Governor Faubus.
Little Rock, Arkansas, 1958.
Costa Manos.

Students watching class on TV.
Little Rock, Arkansas, 1958.
Costa Manos.

**Teacher televising her class
for students barred from school.**
Little Rock, Arkansas, 1958.
Burt Glinn.

Little Rock Central School.
Little Rock, Arkansas, 1957.
Burt Glinn.

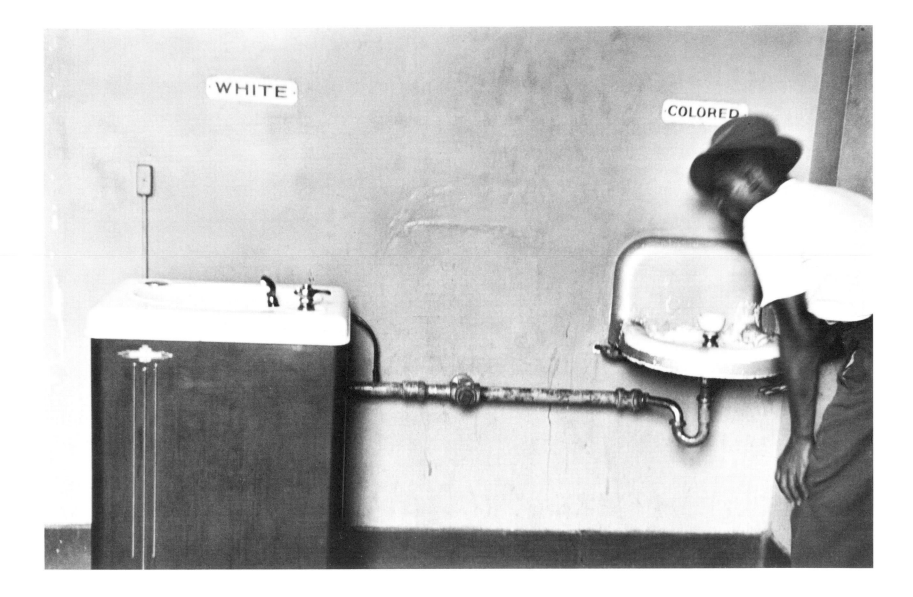

Drinking fountains.
North Carolina, 1950.
Elliott Erwitt.

Road signs.
Georgia, 1959.
Costa Manos.

Ku Klux Klan cross-burning.
South Carolina, 1959.
Costa Manos.

Ku Klux Klan rally.
South Carolina, 1958.
Costa Manos.

Demonstration during final appeals of the Rosenbergs' death sentence.
Washington, D.C., 1953.
Elliott Erwitt.

Rosenberg demonstration.
Washington, D.C., 1953.
Elliott Erwitt.

Rosenberg demonstration.
Washington, D.C., 1953.
Elliott Erwitt.

Rosenberg demonstration.
Washington, D.C., 1953.
Elliott Erwitt.

Senator Joseph McCarthy with aides Roy Cohn and David Schine.
Washington, D.C., 1954.
Eve Arnold.

Alger Hiss.
New York City, 1956.
Elliott Erwitt.

**Pillsbury Bake-Off, high school
students' competition.**
New York City, 1959.
Erich Hartmann.

Pillsbury Bake-Off.
New York City, 1954.
Erich Hartmann.

Pillsbury Bake-Off, high school students' competition.
New York City, 1959.
Erich Hartmann.

FDR statue at Grand Coulee Dam.
Washington, 1953.
Burt Glinn.

Judges, Shriner beauty contest.
Harlem, New York City, 1951.
Burt Glinn.

Entrants, Shriner beauty contest.
Harlem, New York City, 1951.
Burt Glinn.

Tea at the president's house.
Sweet Briar College, Virginia, 1956.
Elliott Erwitt.

Grace Pfost addressing women's group during her Congressional campaign.
Idaho, 1953.
Burt Glinn.

The Du Pont family sits for a group portrait; Irénée Du Pont, left.
Wilmington, Delaware, 1956.
Cornell Capa.

Governor Nelson Rockefeller and aides.
Albany, New York, 1959.
Cornell Capa.

Elizabeth Gurley Flynn, a Communist Party leader.
New York City, 1951.
Burt Glinn.

Pat Nixon's press conference, Republican Women's Convention.
Washington, D.C., 1956.
Cornell Capa.

Joan Crawford, member of the board of Pepsi-Cola.
New York City, 1959.
Eve Arnold.

Gloria Swanson, José Ferrer, and Judy Holliday at the Academy Awards.
Hollywood, 1950.
Burt Glinn.

Grace Kelly after announcement of her engagement.
New York City, 1957.
Elliott Erwitt.

Marilyn Monroe.
New York City, 1956.
Elliott Erwitt.

Marilyn Monroe.
New York City, 1956.
Elliott Erwitt.

Arthur Miller near the Brooklyn Bridge.
New York City, 1954.
Elliott Erwitt.

Showgirl and Eddie Fisher billboard.
Las Vegas, Nevada, 1957.
Elliott Erwitt.

Showgirl and Eddie Fisher.
Las Vegas, Nevada, 1957.
Elliott Erwitt.

Jayne Mansfield and fiancé, Mickey Hargitay.
Los Angeles, 1958.
Wayne Miller.

Wedding of Jayne Mansfield and Mickey Hargitay.
Los Angeles, 1958.
Wayne Miller.

Jayne Mansfield and dog.
Hollywood, 1959.
Inge Morath.

Elizabeth Taylor and Eddie Fisher
being photographed by Sammy Davis, Jr.
New York City, 1959.
Burt Glinn.

John Wayne on the set of *The Alamo*.
Texas, 1959.
Wayne Miller.

Paul Newman at the Actors Studio.
New York City, 1955.
Eve Arnold.

James Dean in Times Square.
New York City, 1956.
Dennis Stock.

Lester Young.
New York City, 1958.
Dennis Stock.

David Amram playing French horn at the Five Spot.
New York City, 1957.
Burt Glinn.

**Allen Ginsberg, Gregory Corso,
and Barney Rosset in Washington Square.**
New York City, 1957.
Burt Glinn.

Gregory Corso in Greenwich Village coffee house.
New York City, 1959.
Burt Glinn.

Poetry reading.
New York City, 1959.
Burt Glinn.

Helen Frankenthaler in her studio.
New York City, 1957.
Burt Glinn.

Helen Frankenthaler and David Smith.
New York City, 1957.
Burt Glinn.

Willem de Kooning with friends.
New York City, 1957.
Burt Glinn.

Van Cliburn after winning International Tchaikovsky Piano Competition in Moscow.
New York City, 1958.
Costa Manos.

Dave Brubeck.
New York, 1953.
Bob Henriques.

Motorama.
New York City, 1953.
Dennis Stock.

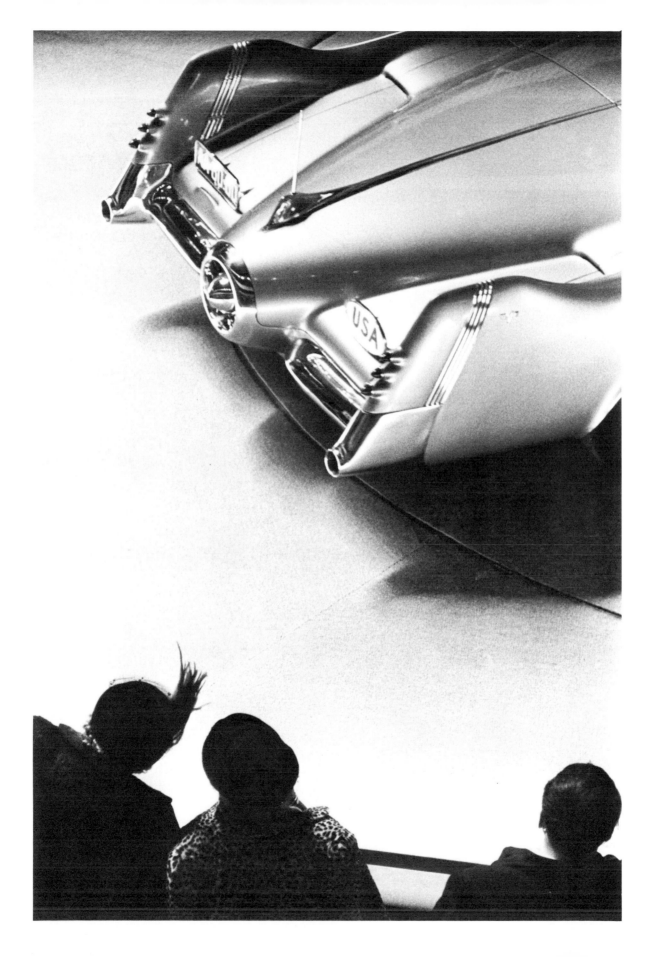

Motorama.
New York City, 1953.
Dennis Stock.

Tailfins.
Westchester County, New York, 1957.
Elliott Erwitt.

Street scene.
California, 1955.
Elliott Erwitt.

Christening the first Boeing 707.
Seattle, Washington, 1954.
Burt Glinn.

Republic Aviation factory.
Farmingdale, New York, 1952.
Cornell Capa.
(*Life* magazine © Time Inc.)

High school cafeteria.
Port Jefferson, New York, 1955.
Eve Arnold.

Sailors on leave.
New York City, 1955.
Burt Glinn.

Marriage-license bureau.
Los Angeles, 1955.
Elliott Erwitt.

June wedding.
White Plains, New York, 1952.
Erich Hartmann.

Swearing-in ceremony.
California, 1950.
Wayne Miller.

USO club.
Seattle, Washington, 1953.
Burt Glinn.

Returned Korea veteran in bar.
San Francisco, 1951.
Wayne Miller.

**Family of soldier killed in Korea,
at ceremony for returned dead.**
San Francisco, 1951.
Wayne Miller.

The first dead from the Korean War.
San Francisco, 1951.
Wayne Miller.

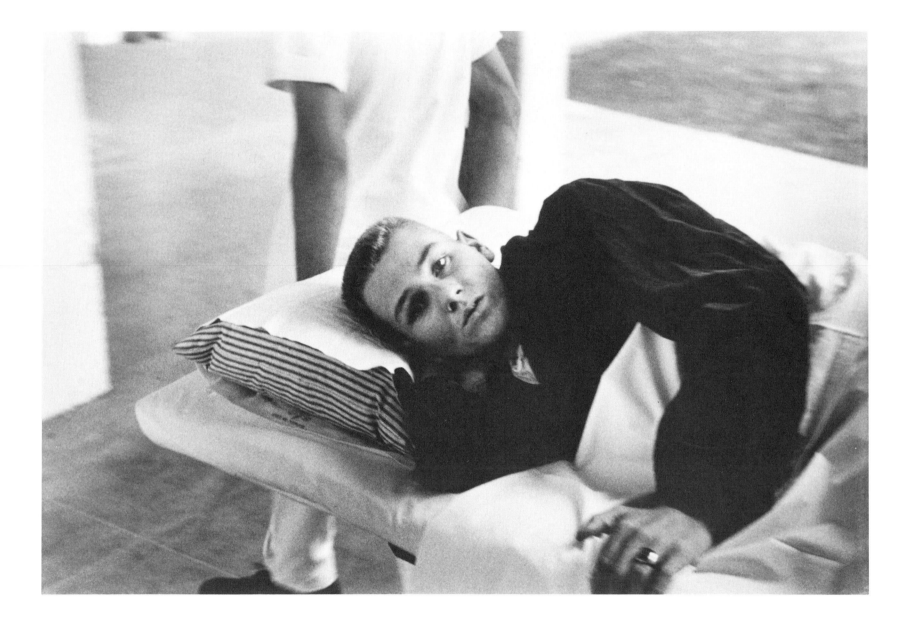

Returned POW in hospital.
San Francisco, 1953.
Wayne Miller.

**Soldier wounded in Korea recuperating
in Travis Air Force Base hospital.**
Fairfield, California, 1950.
Wayne Miller.

Former POW returning to U.S.
San Francisco, 1953.
Wayne Miller.

**General Douglas MacArthur
on his return from Korea.**
San Francisco, 1951.
Wayne Miller.

**Marine from Fifth Regiment
coming home.**
San Francisco, 1951.
Wayne Miller.

Wedding of a returned POW.
California, 1953.
Wayne Miller.

Housing development.
Levittown, New York, 1957.
Burt Glinn.

Signs at city limits.
Fullerton, California, 1959.
Eve Arnold.

Political rally.
Centerfield, California, 1950.
Wayne Miller.

Tobacco auction house.

Wilson, South Carolina, 1956.

Burt Glinn.

Life in a trailer park.
Richland, Washington, 1952.
Wayne Miller.

Migrant workers' camp.
San Joaquin Valley, California, 1950.
Wayne Miller.

Union meeting.
San Joaquin Valley, California, 1950.
Wayne Miller.

Migrant workers' camp.
San Joaquin Valley, California, 1950.
Wayne Miller.

Migrant workers' camp.
Long Island, New York, 1951.
Eve Arnold.

Migrant workers' camp.
San Joaquin Valley, California, 1950.
Wayne Miller.

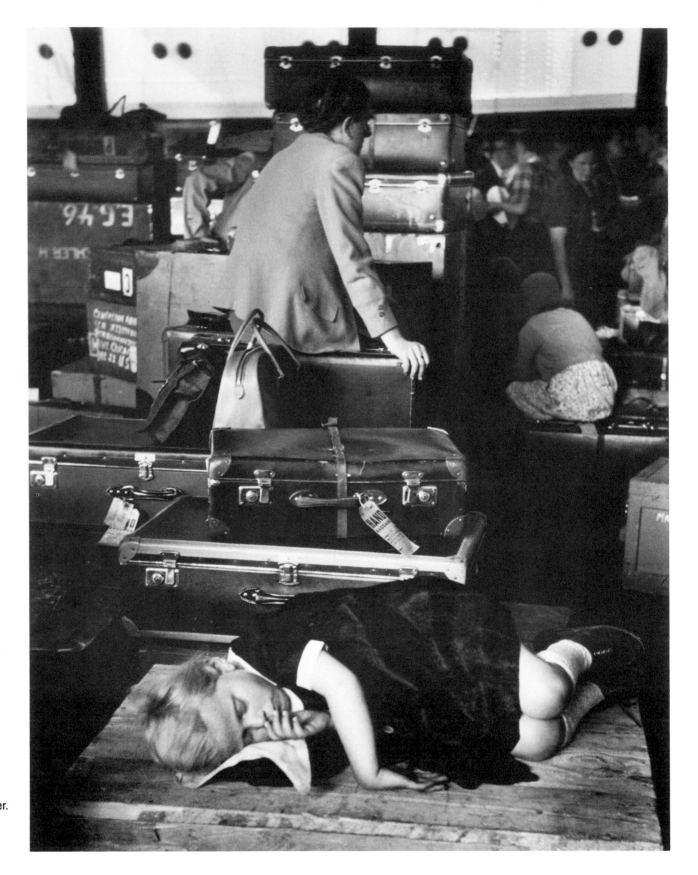

Displaced persons at the pier.
New York City, 1951.
Ernst Haas.

Alien registration.
New York City, 1951.
Burt Glinn.

Unemployment line.
Portland, Oregon, 1953.
Burt Glinn.

Waiting at unemployment office.
Portland, Oregon, 1953.
Burt Glinn.

Older couple living in trailer park.
Richland, Washington, 1952.
Wayne Miller.

Life in a trailer park.
Richland, Washington, 1952.
Wayne Miller.

Gang.
Brooklyn, New York, 1959.
Bruce Davidson.

Gang.
Brooklyn, New York, 1959.
Bruce Davidson.

Gang.
Brooklyn, New York, 1959.
Bruce Davidson.

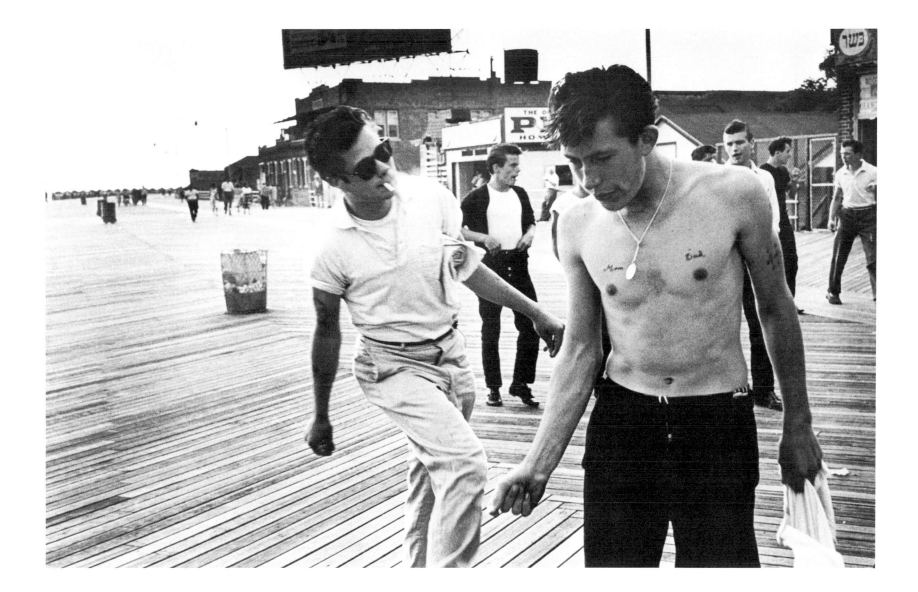

Gang.
Brooklyn, New York, 1959.
Bruce Davidson.

Drive-in church.
Massachusetts, 1951.
Ernst Haas.

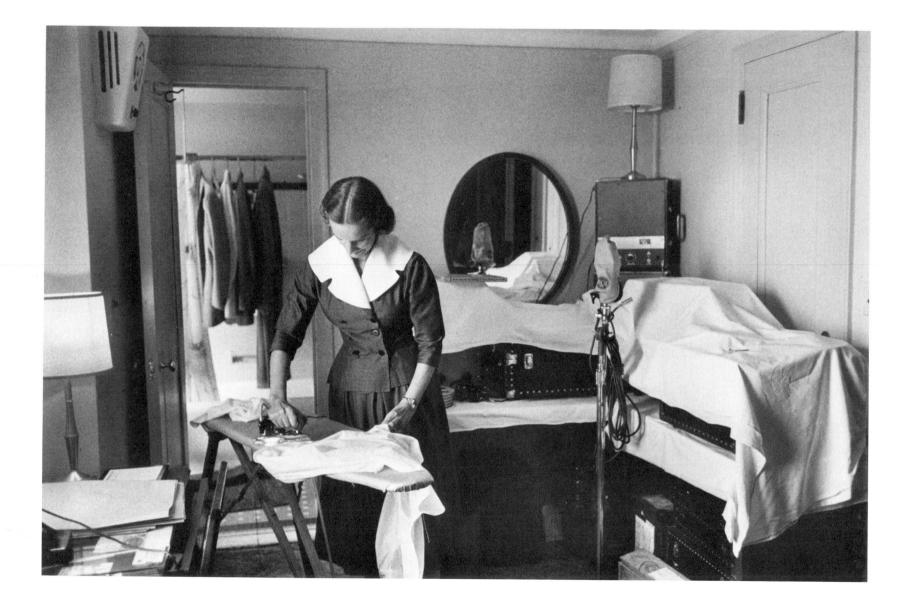

Mrs. Billy Graham in hotel room.
New York City, 1957.
Cornell Capa.

Billy Graham at Madison Square Garden.
New York City, 1957.
Elliott Erwitt.

Oral Roberts at home, with Bible on his chest.
Tulsa, Oklahoma, 1956.
Eve Arnold.

Daddy Grace in his church.
Harlem, New York City, 1959.
Costa Manos.

Mourners.
San Francisco, 1955.
Wayne Miller.

Seventh-Day Adventist meeting.
Pendleton, Oregon, 1953.
Burt Glinn.

President Truman addressing a political rally for Adlai Stevenson.
Hartford, Connecticut, 1952.
Cornell Capa.

Margaret Truman campaigning for Adlai Stevenson; Congressman John F. Kennedy at right.

Lawrence, Massachusetts, 1952.

Cornell Capa.

Former President Truman at Democratic Convention.
Chicago, 1956.
Burt Glinn.

Eleanor Roosevelt and Adlai Stevenson at Democratic Convention.
Chicago, 1956.
Burt Glinn.

Hotel lobby during Democratic Convention.
Chicago, 1956.
Burt Glinn.

Senator Nixon visiting his hometown school.
Whittier, California, 1952.
Wayne Miller.

Senator Nixon working on campaign speech in hotel room.
Upstate New York, 1952.
Cornell Capa.

Crowd watching TV during elections.
New York City, 1952.
Eve Arnold.

Edward R. Murrow.
New York City, 1957.
Elliott Erwitt.

Estes Kefauver, Harry S. Truman, Lyndon Johnson, and Adlai Stevenson on podium at Democratic Convention.
Chicago, 1956.
Burt Glinn.

Henry Cabot Lodge at Republican Convention.
San Francisco, 1956.
Burt Glinn.

Prince Philip, Mamie Eisenhower,
Queen Elizabeth, and President Eisenhower.
Washington, D.C., 1957.
Burt Glinn.

President Eisenhower welcoming Queen Elizabeth at airport.
Washington, D.C., 1957.
Burt Glinn.

Bob Hope, Mrs. Khrushchev, and Frank Sinatra.
Hollywood, 1959.
Burt Glinn.

Louis Jourdan, Nikita Khrushchev, and Shirley MacLaine.
Hollywood, 1959.
Bob Henriques.

**Vice-President Nixon, President Eisenhower, and Premier Khrushchev
admiring Sputnik model at White House.**
Washington, D.C., 1959.
Elliott Erwitt.

Nikita Khrushchev at Lincoln Memorial.
Washington, D.C., 1959.
Burt Glinn.

Nikita Khrushchev and Lyndon Johnson.
Washington, D.C., 1959.
Erich Hartmann.

**Senator John F. Kennedy huddling with other politicians
at Democratic Convention in try for vice-presidential nomination.**
Chicago, 1956.
Burt Glinn.

Martin Luther King, Jr.,
at Prayer Pilgrimage for Freedom.
Washington, D.C., 1957.
Bob Henriques.

Henry Kissinger at Harvard.
Cambridge, Massachusetts, 1958.
Elliott Erwitt.

Newsstand.

New York City, 1958.

Wayne Miller.

**U.S. airman and dog
guarding Matador missile site.**
West Germany, 1958.
Cornell Capa.

Nuclear submarine *Nautilus* in harbor.
New York City, 1958.
Bruce Davidson.

Launching of *Vanguard.*

Cape Canaveral, Florida, 1957.

Burt Glinn.

Watching the Jack Paar show.
New York City, 1959.
Cornell Capa.